Psychological Secrets of Business Superstars Revealed

Smart Biz Guides

Copyright 2010 – Smart Biz Guides

Disclaimer:

CONTENTS

Chapter 1

Introduction

Undoubtedly we live in an age and society of unabashed consumerism. The one and only mantra that drives us is consumerism. Where did this come from? And how on earth, did we become so consumer-driven? The wicked brains behind this are the advertising and marketing geniuses. Advertisements are so evocative and seductive they succeed in putting ideas into heads which would normally not even have thought of them, and then there is no peace until we have finally, and maybe at no small cost, acquired what was being advertised. The real success, though, lies with the people who thought out the whole gimmick. It's the psychological factor they have gained control over. To be a good and effective marketer, therefore, what we need to learn is how to gain that special psychological edge, how to ensure the product is lodged in the subconscious.

There are basically 2 marketing styles:

- Marketing through the mail, and
- Direct contact with people with the hope of making them your customers

Marketing tactics that use the mail have but one aim – to get the person receiving the mail to open the envelope. Then, even if the person is not really interested in what the mail has to say and does not really need the product being advertised, it remains in the subconscious. This kind of subliminal advertising is the most effective. Someday it will surface and give the seller cause to celebrate! And so, how do we get the person to open his mail? Use the right kind of words on the envelope; words that will catch his fancy and his interest. The best way to find the right words is to imagine you are getting mail from an electronics dealer advertising music systems. One dealer, on his envelope has used the sentence: "Fill your home with the sound of music….Gavel Sounds" as their Unique Positioning Statement, or what is known in common parlance as the UPS.

Another company, AWASH, sends you mail which has as its UPS, the following statement on the envelope: "Uncover the secret of having music in every corner of your room with the world's best sound engineers, at a cost that will keep you smiling forever!" It's easy to say which envelope goes unopened into the wastepaper basket, and which one stirs your curiosity. The result, even if you already have 2 music systems at home, you are curious to know about this one, and so, you open the envelope!

In the second instance, you decide to meet people and have one-on-ones about your product with them. Of course experience would have shown you people can be remarkably offhand with sales and marketing executives, UNLESS, their fancy has been caught. To illustrate this point, let us take 4 situations: In each of the cases, the client has been identified. The challenge at hand is to turn the client into a prospective customer. The product being marketed is Brand Ami olive oil.

Situation A:

The seller arranges to meet with the client over lunch at the cafeteria of the organization where the client works. Her conversation is informed. She knows the client only uses quality products, he is conscious of the way the food he likes is cooked, and is a health freak. She talks about the virtues of Mediterranean cuisine and how one can enjoy one's meal just as much when it is cooked in Brand Ami olive oil. What's more, it goes with the current state of health consciousness that aware people are adopting. In passing, she recommends a gym she knows uses the latest equipment in weight training, and has a great trainer.

Situation B:

The seller plans a meeting with the client over a drink after work. When they meet, while the client orders a drink, the seller merely orders a health drink, and starts talking about how important it is to be health conscious. She talks about how using Brand Ami olive oil will help in weight reduction and lowered coronary problems.

Situation C:

The seller takes an appointment to meet the client after work on a Saturday. Without wasting any time, she straightaway starts talking about how important it is to be healthy, eat healthy, live healthy, and almost pushes the panic button on how disastrous it is not to be aware of what medium our food is being cooked in, etc., etc.

Situation D:

The seller has a lunch engagement with the client. He agrees to meet her in a restaurant close to his place of work, and she orders all kinds of health foods cooked in olive oil. Lunch is set and ready when the client arrives and after pleasantries, they sit down to eat. While eating, she broaches the topic of cooking mediums and how interesting cuisine that uses olive oil are. By the time dessert comes, she has finished her sales pitch on Brand Ami olive oil.

Which seller do you think deserves kudos?

The answer is: Seller A. The psychological tactics she uses are sure winners! She knows her client and she knows what she is selling. She is an aware person who uses that awareness to market her product, Brand Ami olive oil.

We know now, without a doubt, when we advertise and market products, we have to keep in mind the psychological factor. So what are these psychological secrets?

Chapter 2

Secret 1: Enthusiasm

For any business venture to be successful, especially something as difficult and challenging as marketing, dollops of enthusiasm are not enough. You need an inexhaustible supply of it. This is because you are not selling a product here, you are in effect marketing yourself. Startling statement that, but true!! When you decide on marketing as your chosen career, make sure you know this fundamental truth. This actually means you have to like yourself and believe in yourself above everything else. Next comes the organization. You have to believe in the organization and what it stands for. And, going further, you have to believe in the products the organization is dealing in. If there is even a fragment of doubt in your mind about either the organization or the products you will be selling, you will never be able to be enthusiastic about your work, and this will immediately show. For it is only when you are totally comfortable with yourself and the work you are doing that you will be able to focus on your clients. People are drawn to you because you are a genuinely nice and positive person, and your enthusiasm just shines through in what you say and your body language. Thus, you build up your network, and clients who you have dealt with will not hesitate to do business with your organization or buy your products. One very important point to remember is it is only when you are totally enthusiastic about what you are doing that your sincerity is revealed. We are not talking here of sophistication or polish - we are just talking about raw enthusiasm. When your clients see how sincere you are, they will believe in what you are marketing. At the end of the day, no one wants to buy poor quality. Remember, while sophistication and polish are very correct, they may not reveal the truth, and for any long-term business proposition, it is the truth that matters. You may be able to fool your client once, but the long-term effects of that can be quite disastrous. You would have compromised not only your integrity, but that of the organization where you work, and the products they sell. The fact is your enthusiasm about the products you are selling instills the feeling of credibility in your customers, for it stands to reason a person who is so enthusiastic cannot be so unless the product she/he is selling is of the best quality possible. And for a client that is important; your credibility is important; your enthusiasm is not something just put on. Your passion is your best endorsement. Your enthusiasm creates a feeling of excitement and enthusiasm in your clients. This is the secret of long-term success.

Check out Anthony Bourdain (famous American author and chef) for sheer enthusiasm in his chosen field of work. His No Reservations on the Travel Channel is an absolute treat. His passion for cooking and food has taken him to all corners of the world. Further, his adventures have enriched his life. The combination is irresistible, and today he is one of the leading culinary experts in the world. His enthusiasm is infectious, his passion is real, and his success is there for all to see.

Another very enthusiastic person, whose life is a real example of enthusiastic perseverance is Captain Brian Iglesias. After 13 years in the Marine Corps, and with a metal plate fused in his neck, he actively pursued his dream of becoming a film maker. He had carried this dream in his heart all through the most difficult of situations. Even after he left the army, he struggled against huge odds to get work as an intern to learn the art and skill of film making. Since no one was ready to give him a break, he decided to form his own company, with help from Entrepreneurship Bootcamp for Veterans with Disabilities, an organization that helps veteran soldiers become entrepreneurs. He, thereafter, launched his company, Veterans Inc., and there has been no looking back since.

To strike out on your own is not easy to begin with. But if you are enthusiastic about fulfilling your dream, no matter what, you will be able to climb and conquer all obstacles that land in your path. In fact, it is precisely this that hones your skills for survival in a dog-eat-dog world and makes you a success.

Chapter 3
Secret 2: Integrity

As a salesman, sincerity is an essential quality - Sincerity to your job, sincerity to your values, sincerity to your customer.

Often, customers operate from the premise that they are going to be cheated. It is only your sincerity that will create confidence in the mind of the customer. He has to believe that what you are saying about the product will stand the test of credibility. And so, you not only talk about and highlight the merits, but also touch on the difficult aspects, not as problems, but as obstacles that the company will help the customer overcome. You are able to tackle any questions your customer might have regarding your competitors, without putting them down, but by showing your own organization up.

A sincere salesman will not take anything personally. He

is doing a job and he is doing it as best as he knows how, and customers always feel and understand that.

One very important thing to remember is that a customer is usually always concerned with after-sales help. If you, as a sincere salesman can convince the customer of this and not glide over it, he will be more persuaded about the product.

You can never push the customer. You have to get him to take the decision. You reiterate the virtues of the product - where the customer would be likely to use this product; that the company would gladly have it installed; and that there were some fringe benefits to this sale.

If you can stand guarantee to your sales pitch, the customer will be completely convinced. He may never get back, but he would have been impressed by your sincerity. If now the customer decides to buy the product, you can be assured that it is only your sincerity that has made him go in for it.

Sincerity of purpose pays off when starting your own outfit. Take a look at gaming. They are becoming more and more realistic, and believable. For example, in the game Warthog, where a Jeep look-alike is used, it actually has wheels. The player actually feels that this is the real thing. A knowledgeable player cannot see anything fake about the game.

If the creator of this game, Alexander Seropian had been anything less than sincere, this would not have happened. Alexander Seropian and Jason Jones launched Bungie, a computer-games company soon after they graduated from college. After 13 years of creating popular games, they sold Bungie to Microsoft. After a stint with Microsoft, Seropian branched out on his own. Using all that he had learnt, and being totally sincere and honest to himself, he started Wideload Games, which is a videogame company. Instead of using the traditional method of developing the software, the model he used is the same as movie production. He chose his team carefully, and kept it deliberately small. He wanted only those who would sincerely and seriously work at finding ways of creating new games that would be authentic and provide value for money. Now he and his team are happy learning, and making a success out of their business.

For a sincere entrepreneur, there are no compromises, no matter how attractive. He thinks long term. He knows that the long-term benefits are mind-boggling.

Chapter 4

Secret 3: Show Sincerity of Purpose

As a salesman, having 'sincerity of purpose' is an essential quality. Picture this scene: You are attending to a customer who cannot make up his mind. You need to make this sale. But you know that you cannot push the customer, because that might be counter-productive. As a sincere and honest salesman, you are trying to get a commitment from your customer. So, what can you do?

You can talk around the question of the sale, such as where the customer would be likely to use this product; that the company would gladly have it installed; that there are some fringe benefits to this sale; that there are so many things that can be done. You would have a honest answer as well to every query. This kind of soft-sell, would eventually lead to the actual sale. You would have made the sale, and the customer would go away knowing he had received a good deal.

Sincerity of purpose pays off when starting your own outfit. Take a look at gaming. They are becoming more and more realistic, and believable. For example in the game Warthog, where a Jeep look-alike is used, it actually has wheels. The player actually feels this is the real thing. A knowledgeable player cannot see anything fake about the game. If the creator of this game, Alexander Seropian had been anything less than sincere, this would not have happened. Alexander Seropian and Jason Jones launched Bungie, a computer-games company soon after they graduated from college. After 13 years of creating popular games, they sold Bungie to Microsoft. After a stint with Microsoft, Seropian branched out on his own. Using all that he had learned, and being totally sincere to himself, he started Wideload Games which is a video game company. Instead of using the traditional method of developing the software, the model he uses is the same as movie production. He and his team are happy learning, and making a success out of their business. A sincere entrepreneur would look out for talent and use it to expand. There would be no compromises, no matter how attractive they looked. This is because for a sincere entrepreneur, the long-term benefits are mind-boggling not only as a person, but also as a business.

Chapter 5

Secret 4: Listening

There is a wonderful story of Gertrude Boyle (Chairman of the Board for Columbia Sportswear). When Gert's husband died suddenly, she was left with Colombia Sportswear, a clothing concern creating clothes for the outdoors. The business was in dire straits. She was faced with a tough choice – either sell the business, for which she would hardly get anything, or try and turn it around. She chose the latter. She pledged all her assets, fired the attorneys and accountants and decided to start from scratch.

The business soared, and then diversified into clothing for women, new designs, and shoes. They also own Mountain Hardware, a company that deals with camping equipment. Her business mantra is you need to listen to your customers, and try to give them what they want in the best quality and design possible.

Listening to customers' demands creates a curiosity about what it is they are actually looking for. Building on that can be hugely satisfying and rewarding. Involving your customers in the creation of a product automatically spreads the word and there is nothing more effective than having your products advertised by way of mouth. Since your customers are involved, there is a huge amount of goodwill generated as well. Gradually you see the product has become financially viable as well. While your own curiosity is making your business grow, advertising your product in a clever way, holding sneak-peaks of your products, stirs the curiosity of people who might come across it.

Certain words can be used to excite people's curiosity such as 'fascinating changes in outerwear', 'warm, cozy and fitting', 'come and improve the style', 'guaranteed style and comfort' and so on.

Curiosity is an inbred thing in all of us, and a good salesman will use this to his advantage. Oftentimes, a customer's curiosity has caused a sale which even he did not know he needed! That is a win-win situation!

Chapter 6
Secret 5: Elitism

Marketing strategies that use elitism as a technique are sure-fire winners. There are 2 major emotions at work in everyone. Everyone wants to feel positive and everyone wants to believe they are one of a kind.

If your product is positive and exclusive or elitist, it is definitely going to be a winner. Given a choice between mass-produced articles of clothing, or shoes, or perfumes, or deodorants, or jewelry, or watches, decorative items, and things that are 'limited editions', nine out of ten people will opt for the limited editions.

Of course, while unethical companies and salespeople try to sell imitations of the original and label them 'limited', the discerning buyer spots it right away and does not fall victim. In the process the low integrity of that particular company becomes public knowledge. However, it is also a known fact that when a really elitist product is created and marketed, it will have a market among those who think highly enough of themselves to know what they want, and are determined enough to get it. People who buy limited editions know they are sure to have something everyone else does not have, thereby putting them in the elitist bracket.

Clever businessmen use their creativity to create new products, new designs, new materials every once in a while, so they can sell to the niche market. Further, increasingly the Internet is being used for marketing, and niche markets are thriving. Not only products, but services are being sold, quite successfully, on the Internet, especially to people who have no access to these where they live.

Customers feel good they are part of a small group that is being exclusively served. The only thing you need is to be aware of what people are looking for. Maybe you are an expert at something and can sell that service/knowledge over the Internet to just a few people. So when you advertise there are only 20 places left for your financial training module, you are sure to get your clients. Or you may have a hobby which you could market on the Internet. You would be creating your own niche market which would be exclusive and elitist.

Chapter 7

Secret 6: Know your competitor

This is of the essence. It is only when you know what you are up against that you will be able to be one-up on your competitor. One cardinal rule to keep in mind is to never put down your competitor, but to make your product, or to see the product you are selling is of the highest quality. In case customers ask you for the difference between your product and another brand, you should be careful how you put the differences across.

Christopher Radko (Ornament designer) accidentally got into the business of creating decorative baubles (Christmas balls) for Christmas trees. When he replaced his family's old Christmas tree stand, it broke and the tree collapsed crushing all the glass-blown ornaments that were on it. Radko was working as a mailroom clerk at that time, but he was determined to replace all the baubles that had broken. He sketched them from memory, and traveled to Europe looking for artisans who would be able to make these ornaments. While on this task, he spotted the biz-op possibility, and got into designing ornaments and getting them crafted, full-time. The way he outdid his competitors was by ensuring his ornaments were exquisitely crafted and of high quality, and by personalizing the Radko brand. He has more than 10,000 designs to his credit, and whenever there is news of his arriving at Macy's or Bloomingdale's, or Saks Fifth Avenue, crowds wait for him to get his signature on their ornaments, and to meet him. Mind you, while most competitors cut their rates to try and get business, Radko's ornaments are not cheap. But, there is a great rush to buy them. There are never any discount on his ornaments, and yet people go for them. Just by maintaining high standards, and his pleasant personal qualities, he has beaten every competitor in the market. He has expanded to include dinnerware and chocolates, but knowing his passion for his work, he will surely beat all competition here as well. There is dinnerware and dinnerware and chocolates and chocolates. You have to know how to beat the competition. And for this there is only one way – know your competitor and be better than him!

Chapter 8

Secret 7: Endorsements

Having high quality products is good, but sales increase quite dramatically if you have been able to get a celebrity to endorse your product.

Celebrities bring that special zing to our everyday lives and most people feel that if this style guru wears this, or so and so uses that, and they too use these products, then a little bit of the stardust falls on them! Often they are not even aware of all the facts about the products. They just take what the authorities have to say about them as the gospel truth.

Celebrity advertising notches up sales as nothing else can, whether it is a perfume, or an acne skin-care cream, coffee, shoes, organic products, green cars, a drink, or crisps. If a celebrity can have it, it must be good! It is the same thing with experts. If an expert goes on TV to say this food is good or that consumer product has no side effects, we blindly believe them.

Of course it helps greatly if the product is really good, and what is being endorsed by the celebrity or expert is what it claims to be. Sometimes, brands engage celebrities at huge costs to endorse their products. There also have been instances when some prospective sportsperson has been used as brand ambassador only because the client saw the potential in the player and used it to his advantage.

People often want to buy an image. For instance, when you have a beautifully physically fit person endorsing a grill, what you are looking at is that beautiful body, and believe if you buy that grill, all the fat will drain off, and when you eat the food grilled on it, you too will get a body like that particular celebrity!

What is happening here is the value is being transferred

from the person to the product that is being endorsed. Of course if the celebrities actually use the products they are endorsing, the credibility of the product goes up. Even something like products from your own vegetable garden can attract celebrities causing your bank accounts to swell. The only thing required is hard work and genuine produce. And you have the Michelin chefs lining up to buy your vegetables and fruits!

Chapter 9

Secret 8: Consistency

This is one of the magic ingredients required if a person wants to succeed either as an entrepreneur or as a salesman. This quality is very difficult to attain and even more difficult to maintain. And yet, without consistency there can be no success at all.

What goes into this? It is ensuring what you are selling is absolutely the same every time. There is not even the hint of a difference.

To prove this point, let's consider a particular restaurant. You have had a wonderful experience. The restaurant had high standards of cleanliness, the staff was attentive, the menu, though not extensive, was interesting, the cutlery and crockery were of good quality, cloth napkins were used, the temperature control was perfect, and the maî·tre d'hô·tel was discreetly present. When the order was placed, he answered all questions knowledgeably about the menu. He knew the ingredients that were used, and recommended changes where he thought the dishes would not match, or about the quantity. He also suggested the wines that would best enhance the meal. The meal was cooked to perfection and served beautifully.

Result: the experience was wonderful. Next time around when you wanted to entertain guests, you thought of the same restaurant. Everything was absolutely the same. Result: the experience was once again wonderful.

If this is the kind of experience you have every time you go to this particular restaurant, what you are responding to is the consistency of the restaurant.

Consistency in everything, even up to the smallest detail. If the restaurant has branches in other parts of the city, or other cities, and if it wants to be as successful as the flagship restaurant, then the entire restaurant right from external décor to internal décor, to the staff, to the menu has to be the same.

How can we acquire this quality? The single most important factor is you have to be sure this is exactly what you want to do. You know this is your forte, and you also know where your strengths lie. You know your weaknesses, and also how best to go about them, maybe by recruiting those who will provide the right foil.

It is hard work to maintain consistency, and one can never rest on one's oars, but it is worth every minute of the hard work and challenge. One way of ensuring there is consistency is by creating a manual with every one's job duties. All staff employed have to go through the same training and grooming process so they reflect the value system of the owner/company.

When Richard Anderson trained and learned his craft with Saville Row tailors Henry Huntsmen & Sons, he worked hard learning the different skills required. Each skill took a minimum of 3 months to learn. This is so the value of consistency would get deeply ingrained, in every single aspect of tailoring. After 25 years, he decided to open his own tailoring outfit on Saville Row. His mantra: to carry on the same time-honored and time-tested techniques with a modern slant. Therefore, as regards quality and service there was absolute and total consistency. Even the method of training apprentices was the same. There was 100% consistency in the core.

What then was different? A little bit of the décor, and arrangement, and in the use of new fabrics and colors. Thus, while maintaining the old, they were able to introduce the new. Their value for consistency allowed them this leverage.

Chapter 10
Secret 9: Accessibility & Comfort

This is mainly for small business ventures that have decided to go solo rather than get into the multiplex shopping bandwagon.

However, today when multi-tasking has become a way of life and the shortest commodity is time, how can we make acquiring what is required for daily living accessible. Also, how can we make the whole experience of marketing a psychologically comfortable one?

The Internet has changed the whole experience of marketing. Since the Internet makes for instant connection with every part of the world, customers now look for instant marketing solutions. It has become possible to sit in the comfort of home and have access to the best consumer items from around the world. So whether it is coffee from Brazil, fabrics from India, wines from France, or books from England, it is all available with the touch of keyboard.

Therefore, for a business to be successful, marketing on the Internet is of the greatest importance. The more attractive your website is, the more people will want to buy from you. Even services such as banking, or getting loans, or buying mutual funds or insurance, can be done online. In order to run a successful business, making use of the convenience of the Internet is a given.

What needs to be done is to find out where there is a lacuna, and then go about filling it. Go ahead and do your own market research. This will give you an idea of what customers are looking for. So, while you can run your own business in a manner that makes it comfortable for your customers, you can expand your scope by using the Internet to access people who are not close enough to come personally to your company/business/outlet. You are thus ensuring your customers have both accessibility and comfortable shopping. Sure winners as a marketing strategy.

In a society where there is cut-throat competition, you need to keep your customers while expanding the customer database. This can happen only if you listen to the ideas the customers come up with to make their shopping experience comfortable and convenient, and use these ideas to improve your business.

Healthcare is one particular area which has made itself accessible to people who live far away from any medical facility. Even medical consultations and medicines and other medical products can be made available.

While talking about accessibility and comfort for customers, good businessmen will also look to improving their own companies by ensuring that employees also have easy accessibility to and comfort at work.

As an example, let us look at Cingular Wireless. This is a large wireless company, but it is sensitive to those customers who are physically challenged. Every individual and every department is geared to helping customers with disabilities. But, Cingular Wireless has gone one step further. Employees with disabilities are fully integrated within the company's workforce. The company is clear on the fact they need talent, and talent is all that matters. If a talented employee has some disability, the responsibility for that employee to work to his best ability is shared by everyone. As a result they have a very diverse program, so their multicultural marketing includes the comfort of everyone – employees, suppliers, community, and customers.

The Wireless Access Task Force encourages their employees and vendors to design and produce accessible products. Every employee is trained to handle diversity issues. They have made their company a win-win one, because while they make the instruments for working accessible to their employees, they make their products and services accessible for all their customers. Even their website demonstrates their seriousness of purpose.

Chapter 11

Secret 10: Principles & ethics

How many salespeople have we heard who have been high on the hyperbole and low on the reality? Many, no doubt. And this is precisely the reason why advertisements are often taken not with a pinch of salt but with the whole jar of salt.

How did this come about? There is only one answer – either the salesman or the company he was selling for had any principles or ethics. So, while short term quick sales may happen with fast and smooth talking, in the long run, the company and the salesman would have earned the reputation of being unscrupulous and dishonest. Let's look at some of the leading companies that use ethics as a business strategy.

Google, as we know is almost everybody's favorite search engine. Yet, in the technology industry, it is hugely influential. This is because right from the very beginning they wanted to conduct all their business responsibly and reduce their impact on the environment. The department that deals with philanthropic obligations of Google.org is resolved to using information and technology to address poverty, disease, environmental issues and disasters.

The company encourages the staff to become involved in all their social responsibility efforts. They never fail to stress the importance of ethical practice to their employees.

While having that cup of mocha at Starbucks, how many of us know Starbucks takes its Corporate Social Responsibilities very seriously. Starbucks' mission statement is about treating all people with dignity, and respecting all differences. These principles are ingrained in everyone who works at Starbucks from the barista to the Board, and includes customers, vendors and shareholders. Having such a vibrant ethics program creates a vibrant corporate culture and makes all their policies, and expectations clear, as well as the flexibility to be competitive.

The United Parcel Service is another example of ethical business practices at work. Since they operate in over 200 countries, this global company with so many languages and cultures provides manuals for ethics in business and code of conduct in 12 languages, so all the employees understand and accept and live the company's ethical policies.

There is the feeling that if a business is run on ethical lines and has principles it is not going to be a success. Nothing is farther from the truth.

One just has to look at some of the largest business houses, those who rake in huge profits, but who use a substantial part of their profits to fulfill their social obligations and commitments. Examples are: Honeywell

International (USA), HSBC (UK), Accenture Ltd. (Bermuda), Nike (USA), BMW (Germany), Cisco Systems (USA), Unilever (Netherlands), General Electric (USA), Precious Woods Group (Switzerland), Fresenius Medical Care (Germany), Accor (France), IKEA (Sweden) to name some corporate houses. All these businesses deliver what they promise. That is the bottom line for them, and they do it in an ethical way. And, they are making profits!

Chapter 12

Secret 11: The fear factor

From an entrepreneur's point of view, there is nothing like fear to spur one on.

Take this example. Bill Wilson had been in the financial industry for 13 years, when one fine morning he woke up realizing he hated his job. In fact, had never liked it and was 42 years old! Fear of and for the future grappled with regret for so many years having been spent doing something he hated.

However, realizing that brooding was not the answer, he talked to a close friend who mentioned there was a winery for sale close by and maybe it would be worth looking into. Bill talked to his brother and sister who encouraged him whole-heartedly. On introspection, though, Bill realized what he was about to do was quite scary. This was hardly the age to gamble with his savings.

Bill's parents agreed to pitch in and the family went to see the vineyard. It was love at first sight. Bill realized now there was no looking back. He was looking at a commitment here! Disappointment hit them right away.

The farmer whose vineyard was for sale changed his mind. But the Wilsons were already thinking and dreaming about the vineyard and working towards acquiring it. Finally, they found another vineyard which had hardly any infrastructure, though it did have the vines. Financially, it was quite a bit on the higher side, as well. By now the whole family was involved. The Wilsons bought the 20-acre vineyard and decided to build their own winery. They put all their collective assets up for sale, borrowed money and got their winery going.

Today, they sell upward of 25,000 cases of wine every year, and have added to their vineyard, so now they have 86 acres of land. 60 acres are under cultivation. The whole family has pitched in offering their various special skills to the business, and each one looks after one special area. Wilson Creek wine is a runaway success! And to think it was born out of fear!!

Fear is also a factor salespeople can use to their advantage. Many potential customers back off from buying a product out of fear. Fear the product is going to turn out differently from what it claims to be; fear they are possibly being overcharged; fear they might not be getting what they were promised; and most importantly, fear they would not be able to get a refund in case there was a problem with the product. It could be a cover for the product being too expensive, or something he can do without, or whether buying that product is a smart thing to do.

This is where all the selling skills of the salesman come into effect. You will need to get under the skin of the customer to decipher what the fears actually mean. Without pooh-poohing the customer's fears, the salesman would be wise to hear out all the fears and objections the customer has, and then patiently, carefully, and objectively answer all questions, and clear up all the doubts and fears using data and facts wherever necessary. Persuasively enumerate all the arguments for making the purchase while removing all arguments against it.

Chapter 13

Secret 12: Persuasiveness

An effective salesman needs to get into the head of his customer. Look at the amount of information we are being bombarded with. As one report puts it, if the kind of information that goes into our head at any point in time were to go into a computer, the hard disk would crash in no time! But, our brains are equipped with a filtering system. It is this filtering system the salesman has to get through. This means the reasons he enumerates to the customer have to be very interesting, very powerful and very captivating, and voila, the sale is made. The marketing message is, in effect, the trigger which sets off a certain kind of behavior.

A customer approaches a salesman with a need for a particular product. Human beings, though, are also driven by desire. If the product they need also fulfills the desire of being something beautiful, something that is one of a kind, something no one in his circle has, something that is unique, then the sale is effective. A good salesman recognizes this.

Now, the information the salesman provides goes through several filters in the customer's mind. The filter of memories: connections with the past flash through the mind's eye. Maybe there have been some bad decisions, which would naturally induce caution, or it may be a good memory, which induces happy thoughts and feelings.

If the advertisement has a famous personality who the customer admires, it adds to happy feelings, feel-good-about-myself feelings; the filter of our values and beliefs: whatever we buy is subconsciously determined by what we feel is important to us. We feel good that we are in sync with our belief system, when we engage in the buying of this particular product. And lastly, there is the filter of the subconscious: this depends on the way we think and process the information being received. It is based on all our past experiences, our intelligence, out analytical skills and our powers of observation and deduction. As both direct and indirect information, perceptible and imperceptible impressions zing through the customer's mind, the salesman very carefully steers the thinking of the customer.

There are some words that aid this such as: EASY – this is a word that immediately relaxes the customer, and removes any apprehension that this product might be a headache. It gives the feeling the product will make life easier and more comfortable; GOOD – a simple everyday word that evokes stability. It offers a feeling of security about the product or service; SAVE – a powerful word which immediately conjures up the image of having what we want and also being able to save money, time, hassles, or trouble.

The product is an affordable proposition; NEW – panders

to our desire to be the first to use this, or first to have this. We feel good about being on the cutting edge of technology; BEST – a wonderful word to persuade the customer that for him only the best will do, or that he deserves only the very best, or the best might cost a little more, but it would be worth every penny. If you back this up with facts and figures, you've made your sale!

GUARANTEED – with this one word, you can remove all fears and clear up all doubts. Buyers love what is called Risk Reversal in marketing parlance. They love the idea of a Money Back Guarantee. Provide the proof the product is good, and give the guarantee, preferably in writing, and the customer is convinced. Thus, since the salesman's persuasive pitch has been based on truthfulness about the product/service, the sheer credibility will cause the customer to process the information and make an informed decision.

First Direct is a great example of persuasive marketing.

The kind of customer service they provide is so persuasive customers do not regret having made the choice of online banking with First Direct. This is because they add a personal touch to their online banking facility. Employees are very well trained to deal with customer expectations. They understand what the customer wants, provide accurate information and guide them through the process required.

Chapter 14

Secret 13: Rapport

The best way to effect a sale whether you are an entrepreneur or a salesman is to establish rapport. If you can do this, you are a sure winner.

Often, what happens is even if a sale has not been made, such a wonderful rapport is built up that a lasting relationship is formed which in turn has other huge benefits.

You would have laid the foundation for networking. Often the first step when building a database of customers through market research is by calling them on the phone. This requires the major ability to listen.

Listening involves hearing the tonal quality of the voice, every inflection in it, and the way the words and phrases are used. This becomes the key for the salesperson and if he uses the same phraseology, it builds up an immediate empathy and rapport.

Once the ice is broken, then the customer can be invited to the store, or the salesperson could make an appointment for an interview. In face-to-face talks, other intangibles come into play such as facial expressions and body language. These also communicate the customer's feelings.

Another important point that influences the building of rapport with the customer is the attitude of the salesperson. A good salesperson will let the rapport build up, and let the talk naturally progress to the product.

Interest in the customer includes finding out a little about the customer's lifestyle. In-your-face sales talk would instantly kill any rapport the salesperson might have succeeded in building up over the phone. The meeting should be pleasant above all, to both parties.

An outgoing, pleasant personality is a magnet and the salesman who has this kind of personality and is genuinely interested in his customers will draw more people to him. This salesman has effectively established rapport with his understanding of the customer's needs as well as his constraints.

At the end of the day, people buy only from people they like, and who they feel are genuine. We've all seen stores where even though there are many counters and many salesmen, people form a line in front of the salesman who has established a rapport with them. They actually don't mind waiting to be served by him, but will not go to another salesman.

In retail, for instance, a salesperson has only about 10 seconds to build a rapport with his customer. Other qualities that create a rapport are courtesy, and patience.

Courteous behavior at all times is a must and patiently

answering all the questions the customer might have are sure to win you sales.

For instance, a salesperson selling Olé, would build up a rapport by discussing the importance of good health, form and fitness; he would find out if there is any history of cardiovascular illness in the family; he would talk about nutrition and the different ways of cooking; he would mention the benefits of olive oil and of how effective the olive leaf extract Olé is.

In the process, the salesperson has established a relationship with his customer and the good will generated helps not only in the sale, but also in expanding the database. This satisfied customer would naturally spread her experience and nothing is more powerful than word-of-mouth advertisement.

Chapter 15

Secret 14: Boldness

No business deal every flourished with timidity. It is only boldness that brings results.

Boldness does not mean aggressiveness, which is unpleasant and highly avoidable, but it means the ability to take risks with a smile.

A wonderful illustration of this is what Hyundai did. They wanted a foothold in the American economy. Their 'Together' advertisement reflected all the basic American values of hard work, gaining respect and giving back to society.

This message went straight for the heart and nothing is more powerful than an advertisement that tugs at the heart strings.

Then, their ever-alert marketing team found out that a multi-year advertising sponsorship for the Academy Awards broadcast was available. Hyundai signed the deal, becoming the show's automotive sponsor for the next 3 years. Along with the high visibility, they had an Assurance plan in place. According to this plan, Hyundai promised to buy back their cars in case their customers lost their jobs or became unable to work. This was an extremely bold step to take when the economy was down. Most auto makers, including General Motors, were in the direst of straits. Hyundai boldly put out 8 Oscar advertisements. Hyundai just about managed to make 10% sales in the first few months of 2009, down from the same period the year before, but importantly, it lured away customers from other brands. Soon, though, its market shares grew and today, it is the 7th largest car selling company.

Additionally, this year they are introducing 3 new models and in 2011, they will have 4 more models in the market.

A huge risk, but in the long run it will pay off, because people will automatically trust a company that can make such bold decisions at a time when everyone around is cutting down.

In effect what Hyundai has done is to see and grab the opportunity provided by the recession. Add to this the fact the last time such a bold step was taken was in 1930 when General Motors stole the limelight from Ford.

Chapter 16

Secret 15: Peer Affirmation

Man is a social animal and social acceptance is a great human need. It is only a very few people who can go against the done and the usual. For most of us, it is important to identify ourselves with other people. We are influenced by the most-visited websites, the most in-demand products, and the most-popular films. Somewhere there is a belief that what so many people are endorsing must be good!

Consumer goods that have the words most-popular on them sell faster than other goods, regardless of the fact it may be inferior to those others.

Human beings, more often than not, want to emulate what others are doing. So, if a salesperson has been able to sell a particular brand of music system to a famous school, using the name of that school he manages to sell his products to other schools as well. The reasoning here is if it is good for the famous school, it must be of high quality!

There are many companies and organizations that get consumers to write slogans about why they chose the goods of these companies/organizations. These slogans are then used as testimonials for further sales, in confidence people will use the same reasoning as those who tried the product successfully.

Consider Apple. For their iPods, they use teenagers and young people who are very hip and in. The message is going across if you use the Apple iPod you are going to join the hip and happening crowd.

Another success story that shows how important understanding the power of peer affirmation is, is about celebrity gardener, Asafumi Yamashita who has his own garden in Chapet, France.

He became a gardener quite by accident. Not finding any satisfaction in his import-export business, he learned the art of bonsai from his parents, and opened his own store to sell bonsai plants. These were the rage in Paris at the time, and everyone wanted a bonsai.

He even sold them to many restaurants and hotels, as well as to private homes. Yamashita was friends with the chef of a Japanese restaurant, Benkey, to whom he had sold his bonsai plants, and when the chef told him how difficult it was to get Japanese vegetables, Yamashita decided to experiment with growing Japanese vegetables such as Komatsuma (a kind of spinach), and Hatsukadadikon (radish).

What one Japanese restaurant used was proof for the others that the vegetables were authentic, and they too started placing their orders for Japanese vegetables with Yamashita. Further, Yamashita was so convinced about the high quality of his vegetables, soon chefs of Michelin-starred eateries were using his vegetables.

What was good for the Michelin-starred eateries would naturally be something really good, and soon Yamashita has a long line of prospective customers. Keeping his garden small ensured his quality never suffered, and thus customers are willing to pay dearly!

Chapter 17

Secret 16: The ability to turn a situation
to your advantage

Both while setting up one's business and while marketing, there is bound to be at least one situation when you have to come face to face with the knowledge there are some things that just do not happen. There are no instant cures for what ails us much as the public would like to believe, but often unscrupulous companies advertise their products/services as if they are the answer to everything. Of course, in order to make a sale, very often such companies throw in something extra. It is not long, however, before the customer realizes he has been taken for a ride. For instance, we often read advertisements from restaurants that say their diners will get a free drink if they opt for the buffet; or, if you buy this particular camera, you will get so many rolls of film free, plus have the happiness of getting them developed free; or this particular cell phone service provider offers so many talk-free hours, so many instant messages for half the rate, etc., etc. However, the discerning buyer sees the hidden agenda in all of them. Most customers, sadly are not discerning, and easily get duped.

For a long-lasting business or sales relationship, it is important to tell the truth. Nine times out of ten, your prospective customers will become your clients when they learn the truth of the product you are trying to sell, simply because they realize you are an honest businessman.

A good businessman throws in his 'freebie' or promises unlimited customer service and care by offering the right advice or putting the customer in touch with the right people. This works especially in the area of mutual funds. When you tell your customers there is no instant mantra for becoming a millionaire overnight, you immediately build trust.

You can build on this by telling them you will help them acquire the tools and the knowledge of how to go about managing mutual funds. You will see, slowly but surely, your client base increases.

Many hospitals advertise because of the stress of life today, people need to be conscious of their physical condition, and they offer heart check-ups. To make the offer more attractive, they add they will have other scans done at the same time, for free. How often we fall into this trap, thinking for the price of one check-up we are getting others done free. In actual fact, it is nothing of the kind.

A sound medical organization and honest medical personnel would go about the whole business without compromising their integrity and promise only that they will help you to maintain good health, but there is no instant cure for anything.

It is possible to turn a negative into a positive, just by approaching it the right way. The truth does sell, contrary to public opinion.

Chapter 18

Secret 17: Instant accessibility to gratification

The Internet is the best example of instant accessibility to gratification. It is within the reach of small businesses, entrepreneurs, and sales and marketing personnel. This is not to minimize the importance of the Yellow Pages or the classifieds in the newspapers. These too offer instant gratification. It is just the Internet is more compatible with the lifestyle of today.

At a point in time when banks entice their customers with credit cards offering all kinds of add-ons and facilities, the business world is cashing in on the use of their credit cards by customers. Products are easily available, and more often than not, free shipping is thrown in.

There is a lovely example about a to-be mother who shops on the Internet for all she feels she is going to need when her baby is born. Since she loves reading, she wants to build up a library for her child starting now. Where does she shop? It is interesting to note that without a second thought she goes to Amazon.com. The Amazon search engine has been designed so cleverly and imaginatively, that when you type in the title of one book, it throws up the titles of other books in the same category. Thus, though the lady had set out to buy 6 books, she ended up buying 24, simply because it was easily available and better still, the mode of payment was so convenient - it assured privacy, complete security, and speed. This is instant accessibility to happiness at its best! What more could a customer want.

Google and Yahoo search engines are so powerful you have almost instant access to everything from the weather to world news, to recipes, to finding long-lost friends.

If a customer is looking to buy a car, all information possible is available on the net. Better still, it is possible to make a comparative study and so make an informed final decision.

E-books are gaining popularity. The customer does not even have to wait for the delivery – it is instant downloading of the book as soon as the credit card payment is cleared, and this takes but a few minutes.

Services dealing with online consultation with specialist doctors, or with financial consultants, or even with spiritual gurus are eminently possible and easily available as well.

The beauty of searching on the Internet is that additional links open up and that literally opens up a world of knowledge.

In 2004, Gord Hotchkiss had spoken of how the world was well on its way to becoming a consumer market where there would be instant gratification for every demand. The Internet would become the point of contact between the customer and the merchant.

If a customer, for instance, is reading about the Dalai Lama on the Internet, a great deal of other information would also be available such as: the various Tibetan Buddhism monasteries; Dharamshala in India where the Dalai Lama has his offices; how to get to the various monasteries; how to access material on Tibetan Buddhism; and Buddhist spiritual practices.

Contextual advertising thus opens up the world. If a customer is looking for an artist, not only is information about the artist available, but you also get a glimpse into his work. Likewise, if you are looking for a musician, you get music and video clips as well. All this helps in the final act of selling and buying.

Go one step further in the movie world. You see a film on the TV. For example, Mama Mia. There is information available on affordable visits to Greece, where you can get yacht rides around the island, and the kind of dress Sophie wore to her wedding. Further, if Pearce Brosnan is your current favorite, all details about all his films and about him are available on the Internet. Before you know it, you are buying videos of all his movies.

When Michael Jackson died, all of his music both audio and video were heavily in demand. Also in demand was the kind of clothes he wore. Since instant availability is the current mantra, stores selling these goods made huge profits.

When companies selling washing machines and microwave ovens advertise there is instant delivery and a person will personally come along to help install it, any customer would prefer to go to that particular company. Additionally, they offer things like a whole set of microwaveable dishes, or scratch-and-win gifts, and the company has people flocking in.

When a customer feels the need for something, he wants that wish to be instantly fulfilled. The company or salesman, who can do this, comes out a winner.

Airline ticketing staff that does online bookings should be able to offer a variety of equally viable options in case one does not work out. These are surefire winners.

Chapter 19

Secret 18: The E to C route

The Emotion to Cash route is one good businesses use. Any company/product/service that uses emotional appeal to make customers feel all warm and good is a winner. They know what people love, and if they can link their company/product/service to that, they know people will buy.

For instance when a national holiday is approaching, using patriotic themes in sales will surely effect more sales. Or, close to Valentine's Day or Christmas or Mother's Day, products that directly appeal to the emotions sell very well. This means the product is speaking to the customer's heart.

All the benefits of the product are being targeted to appeal to the heart. Many emotions are involved here – a feeling of relief that the workload will get easier, leaving time for other things, a feeling of greed, a feeling of warmth that it is something you've been wanting for a long time, and a feeling you will have something your other friends don't have.

So many emotions tumble about in the heart of the customer. An aware salesperson understands this and uses his emotional intelligence to strengthen trust. Through his understanding and empathizing communication, he talks about his accountability, and the reliability of the product.

Perfumes that use art direction, music and story to trigger feelings of passionate love go straight to the heart.

Unique Selling Proposition or USP is fast changing to Emotional Selling Proposition or ESP. An emotional appeal works for consumer durables, services such as banking, and to build popular brands such as McDonald's.

Even the emotion of fear can be used. For instance, if a salesperson takes the line of leading economists World Bank warnings that the best way to save is to invest in bonds because currency is going to crash, that very fear will drive people to buy bonds.

Thus, the salesperson is bringing home the fear of a very perceptible threat, and at the same time showing a way out. Sure winner! Once the emotional angle is taken care of, the features can be explained. The logic would then justify the emotions and wipe away the last traces of hesitation, and the sale gets done.

Chapter 20

Secret 19: Determination

This is a quality that is needed in abundance if an entrepreneur or marketing person has to stay afloat.

Why afloat? Simply because it is when we start out that we are the most vulnerable. We may be determined, but very often things happen to test our determination; test our seriousness of purpose; test our intentions; test us, as it were.

If we can overcome all the hurdles life throws in our path, then we move on and there is no looking back. But we have to remain determined, no matter what. That is the key.

There are so many examples of people having made it big by sheer determination. Let us look at Liz Murray. Every possible card was stacked against her. She was born in the Bronx, New York to HIV-infected parents who were drug addicts, and pitifully poor. Nine year old Liz lived in a filthy apartment with her family. At 16, her mother died, and her father left her. Liz went to High School, but since she had no home, she slept where she could, in the park, or at a friend's house, or in the subway. She didn't allow any of these things to get her down. After graduating from school, she went to Harvard. Liz Murray, today, is an inspirational speaker. No matter what happens, no matter how hard life is, Liz says, one should take life on the chin, go through every battle, and move on ahead one step at a time. No matter what you choose to do, if you are faithful to yourself, and have something you are determined to work towards, you will get there.

Salespeople come up against so many problems. However, determination to know all about what you are selling, gaining knowledge about the market place, and learning how the world of finance works, greatly aids the determination to make a success out of sales and marketing.

One of the big temptations that might come up both for business people and salespeople is to take shortcuts. However, there are no shortcuts to success.

Knowledge is the secret, and there are no shortcuts to gaining knowledge. Know everything about what might even vaguely be an influence on your chosen career. This will fuel your determination to beat all odds. Success is the natural fall-out.

Chapter 21

Secret 20: Clarity

There is nothing more off-putting than woolly talk. While conducting a sale, in a small way, the salesperson is painting a picture of the product he is selling. He is making the customer envision what using the product is going to be like.

To be effective he will need to be very clear. Even if there is some aspect that has not been tested, or for which there is no conclusive evidence, it is better to be clear about it. The clarity in the thinking of the salesperson gets translated into a clear business proposition.

Another thing to be kept in mind is to clearly explain all benefits as well as all results. Remember you are the expert, so you have to know everything about what you are selling. Any subsidiaries that are being used have to be understood by you before you can make your customers understand. And, they will need to understand everything about what they are buying.

Use of specific figures in the data you might be presenting adds to the authenticity of the sales spiel. For instance, it is a good idea to say the brand you are selling is the number 1 brand; or, if you buy 2 products you get a discount of 5%; or while other brands sell 10 oz jars for $15, this brand is priced at $10, though it has the same amount. Data and statistics give a feeling of authenticity, so find out the exact statistics and use them. Remember, no fooling! The right words have a great impact when giving a sales pitch.

Specificity is the mantra here. So, if you are selling bonsai plants, then you must talk to gardeners who are enthusiastic about trying out something new; if you are marketing web designing, then you are targeting creative talent; if it is a certain Naturopathic cure you are marketing for rheumatoid arthritis, then your target is rheumatic patients. Whatever the product, the sales talk has to clearly address what the product is to be used for. General talk only confuses.

Another area where clarity is important is in sales campaigns. A sales campaign happens when a new product is launched, or an old product is being sold in a new avatar. Naturally, to attract sales, a date is fixed mentioning there will be such and such benefit if the product is bought before this particular date.

An alert salesperson, will see if the strategy worked, and if it did, then the date is extended saying due to popular demand the date is being extended, and again, with such and such benefit.

Car sales, for instance, could advertise that if a certain model is bought before such and such date, the car will be serviced free of cost, according to its servicing schedule, until it reaches the 50,000 kms mark. If you are an entrepreneur, then you could say for the first 6 months if the customer has any problem with the goods, it will be repaired or the parts changed free of cost.

Airline ticketing agencies are getting housewives to do their ticketing, by saying just by working from home, they will earn $X a week.

Project coordinators for content writing sites, can earn up to 5% commission on all the projects they get done. And so on. Specific examples bring home the point as nothing else can.

Chapter 22

Secret 21: Pursue your dream

There are two brilliant examples of 'pursuing your dream', which can be a source of great encouragement and inspiration.

J. K. Rowling had a dream: she wanted to be a writer. Right from childhood, she wrote stories, mainly fantasy, which she would read to her sister. After her mother died, Rowling went to Portugal and taught English as a foreign language. Her marriage did not last long, and with her little daughter, Rowling moved bag and baggage to Edinburgh, Scotland. She was unemployed, lived on welfare, and was diagnosed with clinical depression. However, she never gave up her dream, and went from café to café, writing her books. When Harry Potter hit the stands, Rowling's pursuit of her dream against all odds was vindicated.

Another example is Jim Carrey. Jim was born into a family that was initially doing all right, until suddenly there was a downward turn in their finances and situation. They moved to Scarborough, and the whole family worked at the Titan Wheels Factory. Though Jim worked 8 hours a day at the factory, he still went to school. The family moved from job to job trying to keep the family going. They did not even have a proper house, but lived in a camper van.

Jim's dream was to become a comedian, and he never allowed any of his circumstances to cloud that dream. He held on to it, and when he got the chance, he did stand-up routines. He loved it so much he dropped out of school, did gigs, and finally landed a part in 'The Duck Factory', a sitcom. In 'Living Color' was a hit, and that led him to parts in 'The Mask' and 'Ace Ventura'. He is one of the greatest comedians today.

Dreams have a way of becoming real if you hang on to

them long enough and hard enough.

Chapter 23

Secret 22: Appreciation

This is the universal stimulant, invigorant and pick-me-up tonic. Appreciation of yourself spurs you on to do better and better, while appreciation of your customers, not only makes sales happen, but builds life-long relationships.

Appreciation is good for you and good for your business, whether it is your own business or a sales job.

The world has become unbelievably high-tech, and it seems to be getting more and more technology-oriented by the day. A lot of sales happen online, so there is no human contact at all.

Yet, it is a known fact it is people who sell. If the customer likes a salesperson or a business man, he is more than willing to do business with them, as compared to an automated response to queries, or getting connected to formless, digital sounds that do not really help.

While there may be room for this, good business practices still use the human factor. After the sales talk is over, keeping in touch through instant messaging or texting to inform potential customers there is some new development in the product, or there is some expert coming to the showroom and is ready to field questions and give advice, maintains the human contact. 'Thank you for attending' messages help show appreciation.

Appreciation Marketing is very popular only because there are follow-ups for every meeting, or after every meeting. Mind you, keeping in touch through messaging or texting is not only to remind the customer the payment installments are due, but also to acknowledge payments received.

Many restaurants keep their clients by remembering their birthdays and anniversaries, and either sending flowers, or offering a complimentary bottle of wine for a special meal in their restaurant.

There is a touching story of how appreciation helps keep a company in everyone's consciousness. Mr. John Pierson owns the local Toyota dealership at Stuart, Florida. He makes it a point to be involved in the community and is very appreciative of everything that happens there. To celebrate their mother's birthday, a family had planned a whole day outing for her. The last stop was at the Kilwins Ice Creamery. Though the birthday lady protested she had had too much to eat the whole day and did not want any ice cream, she wanted to get her granddaughter some. However when they went in, they were told the whole treat was on Mr. Pierson. He had remembered the lady's birthday! And, thanks to him, everyone at Kilwins at that time got a treat!! No matter what the occasion, Mr. Pierson always has a hand in the celebrations. His appreciation of the community where he lives has made Toyota a household name there.

Human beings thrive on appreciation, and good sales strategy uses this to advantage.

Another strategy uses words which make the customer think he is smart. Harmless flattery, no doubt, but powerful in effecting sales.

People feel Valentine's Day is a commercial venture. This is because the 'just for your Valentine' tags cater to that deep need for appreciation and validation we all have.

Banking services that use the 'for preferred customers' are using Appreciation Marketing. Hotels which have 'Preferred at the Park' (for instance) memberships, make the people who get this membership feel special, and consequently make them loyal customers to these organizations. Naturally, they offer special features that are not available to the non-members.

Making the person who has just concluded a sale feel good about his product can be done by sending a congratulatory message to him.

Astute advertising is all about making the customer feel intelligent, savvy and smart if he should go in for this particular brand or service. Remember, a person receives so many messages advertising products and services, that 9 times out of 10, he deletes them without even reading them. How then can you reach such a customer? Only by sending messages worded such that you give the customer the feeling there is no hurry, and he can take his time deciding, but you will be available to furnish whatever information he might need.

Newsletters help to maintain the contact too. However, here again, it is important to see to it that after reading it the customer is not put-off. There should be information about the product, and the possibility of good deals for the 'smart and savvy'.

A good way of keeping in touch is by offering free maintenance and check-ups. That way when the customer drops in, you can tell him about all the new developments, and by showing an interest in your customer, he continues to maintain his relationship with you and the company you represent.

Chapter 24

Secret 23: It's about more than money

It's about the intoxication of making an idea work. It's also about not allowing failure to get you down.

Nicholas Hall is founder of Startupfailures.com. This is a community website where people share the challenges of their entrepreneurial ventures, and which Hall uses to encourage and advise people who have failed to get back on track. According to him, entrepreneurs should know where their forte lies – is it in turning failing companies around, or is it in developing new ideas, but not being able to handle day-to-day tasks. He is a self-styled serial entrepreneur who wants to make things better, and develop new things. He believes it is possible to bounce back from any failure, provided you are willing to learn from that failure. B-schools help you build your network, but when you are in the real world, then it is sheer guts and mental strength that carries you through.

Every entrepreneur has to know that on the path to success there are many, many failures. Microsoft, and Apple too, had many, many failures.

Paradoxical as it may sound, it is the failures and the 'no's that drive and sustains the enthusiasm and energy.

The worst words that can cross your mind are 'I quit'. It is far more important to hang in there, because you never know when you will strike gold. But, the rider is you should have learned from your mistake.

The successes are temporary, the failures are temporary. The only thing that is permanent is the learning, the happiness of learning. When you stop pursuing success and just enjoy the journey, success happens.

According to Hall, the only and biggest hurdle is self-doubt. Self-doubt is self-defeating, and worse you lose your focus, worse still you feel you have wasted precious time and money, and are a loser, and worse and worse is the fact you become completely negative, mentally fatigued and blocked up. If you, instead, focus on the joy that comes from learning, the money will take care of itself.

Chapter 25

Secret 24: In your own area of work,
become a social entrepreneur

Stef Wertheimer, an Israeli industrialist has his own way of reducing conflict in the Middle East. Leaving school at 14, he started making weapons for the Jewish underground forces. Four years on, he started designing and making small industrial tools. His kitchen was his workplace. He delivered these tools on his motorcycle. In 1967, France put a weapons embargo on Israel. The Israeli Government commissioned Wertheimer to make blades for their fighter jets. Iscar Metalworking was thus born. This was where industrial precision metal-cutting tools were manufactured. Today Iscar has operations in Asia and Europe. He, however, came to believe the only way to diffuse war was by providing jobs for people.

Economic prosperity would solve problems that war was never going to. It was this belief that caused him to start an industrial park, Tefen. When Warren Buffett acquired stakes in Iscar, he said that Iscar and Tefen Industrial Park were examples of how people could work against the odds.

Wertheimer never took any help from the government. He had a vision of creating, in his own way, a productive and economically independent society. He encourages young entrepreneurs to work in his park and by making it possible for entrepreneurs to get a foothold, he has advanced the cause of peace.

It is possible to, with sheer grit and courage, make your vision come true. Only you have to believe. Wertheimer need not have shared his wealth, or the secrets of his success. But, his sense of responsibility to his country, and his realization that war did not solve any problems, jobs engendered peace, and brought economic stability to the people and the country, were forceful enough to launch his ventures in social entrepreneurship.

Chapter 26

Secret 25: Use the chances

Very often chance happenings can change your life. You have to be attuned to these chance happenings. When you turn a poor hand of chance into a winner, it is called Luck.

Bob Williamson calls himself an accidental entrepreneur. At age 17 he walked out of his broken home. He hitchhiked around the country and at 24 years of age arrived in Atlanta, a junkie, broke and homeless. He got himself a job cleaning bricks at $15 a week. Soon after getting this job, Bob was in a car accident. In the hospital, he read the Bible, and decided he wanted to make a clean break with the past and do something with his life. However, he was faced with two dreadful facts: he had a criminal record, and he had no college degree. Finally, he got a job at the Glidden paint company, putting labels on cans of paint. He created his work mantra: 'First one there and last to leave.' He worked hard and got the company to computerize itself. He changed jobs, and gradually, became an expert in paint. To facilitate his hobby of airbrush art, he experimented with paints and made paint with a new formula. This was such a success, he soon started his own paint company, Master Paint Systems. His need to expand was so strong he branched out into other businesses, and kept on learning and adding to his fund of knowledge.

When he realized that for good business, he needed systems, he got together a couple of software programmers and they wrote out software for the different companies. His troubles were far from over. In an audit, he found an accountant had been embezzling money for years. Instead of filing for bankruptcy, he decided to fight to recover his company. He took his creditors into confidence and while urging them not to file lawsuits against his company, he sent them letters every week telling them about all that he was doing to get his company back on track. Painstakingly, Bob rebuilt his company, and in fact took it further. He then sold all his companies and started Horizon in 1992.

He then focused on creating systems and writing software for organizations like school cafeterias, hospitals, nursing homes, colleges and military bases.

Though Horizon is a more than $40 million company, Bob is still the first one at work, and the last to leave. He says he saw the chance in situations and took them – the accident that gave him a chance to change his life, the chance formula he discovered for his paint, the chance exposure to creating software. He took them all, and with hard work, he converted those chances into success.

Chapter 27

Secret 26: Love what you do, and focus on it

Jim McGown, a degree holder in pure Mathematics from the University of Miami, and a successful real estate developer, stockbroker, and mortgage broker, suddenly decided one day that he wanted to do something that he has always loved: To become a traditional piazzaiolo.

He bought an Irish pub, renovated it and restored the 19th century Neapolitan brick oven. He put the word out that he wanted to learn how to make pizza the traditional way.

Retired pizzaiolos found his enthusiasm infectious and taught him the art. McGown took to it like a duck to water. Blissfully happy, he learned all about the dough, what temperature is required for it to rise, and the hundred little things the experienced pizzaiolos taught him. The restaurant became such a hit people were traveling from far-off places to check it out.

McGown had his share of failure when his venture with a Yacht Club failed. He learned then that for a business to succeed, you have to know the market. A simple lesson learned the hard way.

Now with South Brooklyn Pizza, he is focusing only on what he knows to do best. So instead of an extensive menu, his eatery serves only one kind of pizza – the classic Margherita which he serves on proper oak boards. He added oven-baked chocolate-chip cookies to his repertoire. McGown's pizzas and chocolate-chip cookies are something to die for, they are that good. His secret recipe is to keep things on a modest scale but offer the very best.

Another story of a person changing lanes is about the sales manager of Mazda cars in Oman. A doctor by profession, P. Kumar could not suppress his love for cars. Without any kind of formal training in sales and marketing, all he had to recommend him was his love for cars and his knowledge about cars. He was put on the lowest rung of the sales and marketing group of Mazda cars. During his interaction with prospective customers, he transmitted his love for cars to those he served. His success was such that soon he was heading the sales and marketing division of the automobile center. Not only this, but Kumar preserved a lifelong relationship with all his clients through the years. As a result whenever they wanted to exchange their car for a newer model, it was this salesman the clients asked for. No matter how high up he went in his sales career, he always had time to be on the shop floor interacting with customers.

Chapter 28

Summing Up

To round off our Secrets, let us sum up what they actually mean:

Dream, recognize your dream, and decide to make it come true

Make yourself knowledgeable. Check out the subsidiaries that go with it, too, so that you equip yourself with in-depth knowledge about everything directly, indirectly and remotely connected with what it takes to make your dream come true.

Recognize the challenges (not problems) that crop up, face them, understand them and work them out. Each has an inbuilt solution which will go toward making your dream work.

Remember, perseverance and determination are your mantras.

Communicate clearly, first with yourself, then with others. Whether you are trying to build a customer base by approaching prospective customers first on the phone, and then in person, or by doing market research, or by giving presentations, organize all the material you have gathered and be well-prepared to answer all queries. Your preparedness will be reflected in your confidence., and confidence attracts customers as nothing else can.

Use the PREP formula as a guideline: this is the Point-Reason-Example-Point formula. Use this for yourself first. For instance, P-walking alone is important for me, R-because I feel strong and focused through the day, E-I can take on any challenge, and find the solutions, P-that is why I love the exercise and the solitude of walking alone every day. Use it for the product you are selling. For instance, if you are selling laptops, P-Spot-on

Technologies has made improvements in their latest model of laptop so it has become even more user-friendly, R-this is because more and more people are wanting instant information, E-of course we are also developing our own search engines which will help with instant accessibility, plus we are trying to make the laptop smaller and lighter for greater convenience, P-we've always had 100% success with all our ventures, and there is no reason we will fail in this one. When you use this formula, it clears up thinking, and this is what is important. You have to be very clear about what you are trying to say. This will make your communication precise, concise, to-the-point and attractive

Listen carefully to your customers. You might be able to pick up some tips besides, of course, the fact that everyone loves a good listener.

Be courteous, polite and very appreciative. These are attractive qualities. Also, be consistent in your dealings with people. It builds confidence in your customer.

Have celebrity endorsements, as well as peer endorsements. The I-would-like-to-have-what-they-have syndrome is quite potent.

Never ever compromise on your ethics and principles. There are no short-cuts in life, so going after them will only end up in your wasting more time than if you pursued excellence in your chosen field of business or marketing.

Love what you do. Don't get carried away by success, but stick to what you know best and do best, and you cannot fail.

Chapter 29

Examine and Review

It is time to rate your business, sales and marketing techniques. Remember this is a self test, and so the key word is HONESTY. It is only when you face yourself honestly, that you will know which areas need to be changed, which need fine tuning, which areas need to be overhauled and maybe re-worked.

As you answer these questions, you can rate yourself on a scale of 1 to 10. Alternately, you can jot down your findings, and use that as a blueprint.

A)Do I love what I am doing? Am I enjoying myself?

B)What are the changes that I need to bring about in my style of functioning?

C)What best practices do I need to incorporate?

D)Have I compromised on any of my principles?

E)Did I do all that I could?

Of course for every answer where you feel you have done your best and have the results to prove your efforts, give yourself a Hi-5!

1.On ENTHUSIASM

a.Are you comfortable with yourself?

b.Are you excited about the work you are doing?

2.On INTEGRITY

a.Have you have enough knowledge about your product and the subsidiaries?

b.Have you ensured that the product you are selling is the best, and not spurious?

c.Have you spent enough time with the customer explaining the product?

3.On SINCERITY

a)Did you have to make compromises?

b)Did you do a soft sell, or are you aggressive?

4.On LISTENING

a)Have you actually listened to your customers?

b)Have you incorporated, or got the company to incorporate the changes you believe will be good, or which make sense?

5.On ELITISM

a)Did you market a really authentically different product, or did you indulge in a copied version?

b)Did you make your customer feel special?

6.On KNOW YOUR COMPETITOR

a)Did you indulge in competitor bashing?

b)Did you work out/offer concrete ways of making your product one-of-a-kind?

7.On ENDORSEMENTS

a)Did your product match, truthfully, the endorsement you were able to get from a celebrity?

b)Are you sure what you are selling is genuine?

8.On CONSISTENCY

a)Were you consistent in your claims? Is there consistency in your product?

b)Were you consistently courteous and polite, even when the customer chose not to buy your product?

c)Do you know where your strengths and weaknesses lie? How do you plan to go about them?

9.On ACCESSIBILITY & COMFORT

a)Is your store accessible?

b)Are you making it comfortable for your customers to do business with you?

c)Are you ensuring the comfort of those who work for and with you?

10.On PRINCIPLES & ETHICS

a)Are you a responsible businessman/salesperson?

b)Do you have a clear-cut vision of how you want to run your business?

c)Do you have convictions that you abide by, no matter

what?

d)Have you had the temptation of doing a quick sell?

e)Do you believe ethical practices result in real profits?

11.On THE FEAR FACTOR

a)Have you used the fear factor to your advantage by taking up a prospect as a challenge?

b)Have you negatively used the fear factor with your customers, in trying to get one-up over your competitors? Or have you heard out their fears, and done what you could to allay them?

12.On PERSUASIVENESS

a)Has your persuasiveness been based on truthfulness?

b)Are you prepared to faithfully do all that you have promised?

13.On RAPPORT

a)Do you believe that it is important to build up a rapport with the customer?

b)Is it necessary at all? Especially if you know your job?

c)The time spent in establishing a rapport with your customer is time well spent? Elaborate how you did this. Or did you not?

14.On Boldness

a)How did your efforts at marketing show boldness as opposed to aggressiveness?

b)Could you take on the risks that you foresaw, calmly and smilingly, without becoming aggressive?

c)Would you recommend that boldness is required in any business/marketing venture?

15.On PEER AFFIRMATION

a)Peer affirmation is important. What are the strategies you would formulate for using peer affirmation as opposed to the strategies for showing the product is for the elite only?

b)Would you sell off a sub-standard product just because it has peer value?

16.On THE ABILITY TO TURN A SITUATION TO YOUR ADVANTAGE

a)There are many products we know cast a spell. They have the allure, but there is a fine print which you as the salesperson are aware of. Would you honestly bring this to your customer's notice? Or would you let it pass?

b)Did you make the in-built negative seem as if it were merely a challenge?

17.On INSTANT ACCESSIBILITY TO HAPPINESS

a)How often do you refine and retune your methods of providing instant access to your customers?

b)Are you ensuring you are aware of all the subsidiaries that are available to make the experience of buying and selling a more complete one?

18.On THE E to C ROUTE

a)Have you made an in-depth study of how human emotions work?

b)Have you been able to truly empathize with your customers?

c)Did you have all the material necessary to show alternative paths?

19.On DETERMINATION

a)Were you able to make a cool-headed assessment of all the odds you were up against?

b)What is the one single thing required to fuel determination?

c)When one plan failed, did you work on another plan to better the first one, and put it in place? Or did you allow yourself to be paralyzed by the failure?

20.On CLARITY

a)Do you check regularly to see if the clarity of your vision is intact?

b)Is specificity important for clarity?

c)If the customer has caught you on the wrong foot, would you honestly agree, and tell him you will get back as soon as you are sure of the facts. After which do you, actually do that most difficult of tasks which is, get back to the customer with the answers/data he wanted?

21.On PURSUE YOUR DREAM

a)Are you following your dream, or living someone else's?

b)If you find there is something blocking the realization of your dream, would you work your way around it? Or opt out?

22.On APPRECIATION

a)Is this real value with you?

b)Would you agree that appreciation starts with you?

c)Is it necessary to be appreciative of the staffs who work for and with you?

d)How would you rate Appreciation Marketing as a useful strategy?

23.On IT'S ABOUT MORE THAN MONEY

a)Is it really about more than money? Isn't it just about making a sale?

b)When failures come along, how often do the words 'I quit' cross your mind? And how often do the words 'I am bigger than this problem' cross your mind?

24.On IN YOUR OWN AREA OF WORK BECOME A SOCIAL ENTREPRENEUR

a)How responsible do you feel towards the society you live and work in?

b)No one is unimportant. Do you believe you have something to contribute? How are you fulfilling that? Give concrete examples.

c)How important is the environment factor in a manufacturing/sales proposition?

25.On USE THE CHANCES

a)How would you rate your awareness quotient?

b)Do you consciously take advantage of the chances that pop up on your path?

c)To turn chance to advantage, you have to have faith in yourself. Do you honestly feel you have faith in yourself? If not, do you have the grit to work towards it?

d) Have you learned from your chances?

e)Have you used what you have learned to better your business/sales products/techniques?

26.On LOVE WHAT YOU DO AND FOCUS ON IT

a)You wake up one morning to see you no longer want to be in sales. You'd rather be a restaurateur. Would you be able to make the switch?

b)Is it important for you to be the best in your field of expertise?

Chapter 30

Some more Tips you can use:

1.Banish complacency. Keep adding something new to your business or to your marketing style. In case you have included something new in your business, such as a new product, or have expanded, or have added a service, immediately make it known to all who are on your database, and also by advertising in venues that are popular. Make sure your website is updated regularly as well, since the number of people shopping on the Internet is increasing by the day. When services are added to businesses, the whole proposition immediately becomes more attractive, and you will see a substantial increase in sales.

2.Become a resource person. There is nothing more potent than knowledge and information in becoming a successful businessman. Offer that information and knowledge freely to those who come to you. In fact, if you can find ways of helping your customers do things in a faster and easier way, you would be helping them save money. This would translate into their doing more business with you. Look for opportunities, look for lacunae, look for the gaps you can fill.

3.Offer value-ads. Customers should know if they do business with you, they not only get what they want, but get more.

4.Offer pain-free solutions and prompt customer care. When customers buy consumer goods, no matter whether it is a car or a kettle, they want to know if they will be assured of after-sales service. If you are offering a service, the single over-riding factor why customers will come to you is if you promise them there will be no after-the-service problems. In fact, people are willing to pay more if they know the service you can provide is totally hassle-free. If you are a medical health practitioner, your clients will be attracted to your clinic if they know the whole experience of coming to you will be a good one from all respects.

5.Keep your antennae buzzing. If you are in it and with it, you should be able to keep up with all the new things that are happening. Take advantage of these new developments, especially in the field of Information Technology, and see how best to incorporate them into your business. Gone are the days when you could do the same thing year in and year out, and be none the worse for it. Change is the new mantra and there is every opportunity for change and improvement and progress.

6.First impressions last. These first impressions are make-or-break moments. There is a clear connection between confidence levels and customer acceptance. If you inspire confidence in your customers, with a positive first impression, you have a stronger chance of being accepted. It would even be considered worth it if you apportioned a part of your capital to hire a professional to create that first impression either in your logo, or website, or brand name, or even your store.

7.Draw from others. Read success stories. No one likes to talk about or dwell on their failures. But you will find enough material in biographies and autobiographies of successful businessmen to draw inspiration.

8.Exude calm strength. Use only those colors and objects that create a soothing atmosphere. Ambiance is extremely important for any kind of business.

9.Always have your venture in your mind. Eat it, sleep it, dream it and talk it at every opportunity. The best way to do this is to have every thought and plan and idea penned. Then, your memory will never fail you. From your scribbling will emerge the picture you want. This has another very practical value. In case you run short of funds, you will be able to explain clearly what your business interest is and how you are going about developing it. No financial institution will give you a loan unless they are convinced.

10.Always meet deadlines, preferably beat deadlines. Your customers and clients will take you seriously if you honor all deadlines. Obviously this might involve sacrifices, which you will have to gladly make. Keep your professional life and personal life separate as much as is possible.

11.Don't use any words that exude negativity either to yourself or to your clients. Any 'failures' should be treated as learning experiences. Keep the larger picture in your mind at all times. Remember, always keep your shoulders squared, chin up and look life in the eye. You can't stay down then!!

12.ENJOY!! This is the most important tip. In all your hard work, in all your profit-making, in all your learning experiences, don't forget that most necessary and most significant ingredient of all – to have fun and enjoy yourself. If you can enjoy what you are doing, your creative juices will run, and the positive energies you exude will draw more positive things towards you.

13.Surround yourself with those who are supportive. Further, don't allow yourself to be discouraged by what anyone says or if something does not turn out the way you want it to.

14.Be flexible. There is nothing wrong in changing/refining/redoing/recharting your course of action. Remember, if you are not flexible, you will break. Also, be flexible to accommodate what your customers want. Maybe they are looking for subsidiary products or additional services. Be prepared to get it for them. A secret is to never say no, but that you will try your best to see that their wishes are accommodated.

15.Train yourself. It often comes as a surprise to

businessmen that there are other aspects to a business like bookkeeping, IT-support, advertising and marketing. Learn all these skills. That way even if you hire people, you will be fully cognizant of what they are doing.

16.Network. This is the secret of success. It works both ways, and all concerned benefit.

17.Set aside time for yourself every day. No matter what the pressure, or how great the demands on your time, you must set aside a little time for yourself to review what you did and what all happened.

18.Allow yourself to grow. It can be a frightening feeling, but it is necessary. Stagnation kills, so spread your wings and fly. Expand your knowledge.

19.Develop a hobby. If you don't already have a hobby, it is a good idea to develop one. It is imperative that you get away from your work and do something you like, or cultivate something you have long wanted to.

20.Speed of response. This is very important in any venture. Confirming orders and getting back to the customer when you have to, always pays.

Chapter 31

Nuggets of Wisdom

1.Three mantras for success according to Zig Ziglar are optimism, patience and hard work.

2.Norman Vincent Peale: 'It's always too early to quit.'

3.According to Pierre Teilhard de Chardin, we have 'to proceed as if limits to our ability did not exist.'

4.Walt Disney: 'If you can DREAM it, you can DO it.'

5.Erica Jong believes that 'if you don't risk anything, you risk even more.'

6.'Social entrepreneurs are not content just to give a fish or teach how to fish. They will not rest until they have revolutionized the fishing industry.' Bill Drayton

7.Henry David Thoreau was of the opinion that castles were meant to be built in the air. 'Now put foundations under them'!

8.Great inspiration from Thomas Edison, and a beacon for everyone: 'I have not failed. I've just found 10,000 ways that won't work.'

9.For all entrepreneurs who are beset with doubt as to why they went in for entrepreneurship in the first place, Guy Kawasaki has this to say: 'The best reason to start an organization is to make meaning - to create a product or service to make the world a better place.'

10.Lisa M Amos: Entrepreneurs average 3.8 failures before final success. What sets the successful ones apart is their amazing persistence.

11.On how important it is to know your competition, Jay Abraham has this to say: 'If you're attacking your market from multiple positions and your competition isn't, you have all the advantage and it will show up in your increased success and income.'

12.It is every businessman's/salesperson's dream that his customers come back. The secret according to John Ilhan is that 'you need to give customers what they want, not what you think they want.'

13.Stuart Wilde: 'The point to remember about selling things is that, as well as creating atmosphere and excitement around your products, you've got to know what you're selling.' And that is the bottom line!

14.From Konosuke Matsushita: 'Authentic marketing is not the art of selling what you make but knowing what to make, of creating solutions that deliver satisfaction to the customer, profits to the producers and benefits for the stakeholders.

15. A powerful quote from John D. Rockefeller: 'If your only goal is to become rich, you will never achieve it.'

16. According to Harry Truman, 'Men and women who got to the top were those who did the jobs they had in hand with everything they had in energy, enthusiasm and hard work.

17. Ryan P. Allis: 'Find a niche market opportunity, exploit it, then reap the benefits while at all times searching for your next niche to enter, move to make and edge to employ.'

18. How important it is to cultivate yourself when going in for entrepreneurship or a job in sales and marketing is given in the words of Bo Bennet: 'Success is not in what you have, but who you are.'

19. It is a complete fallacy that one has to be selfish in business. Brian Tracy says that: 'Successful people are

always looking for opportunities to help others. Unsuccessful people are asking, what's in it for me?'

20.Jim Rohn inspires with the words: 'If you are not willing to risk the unusual, you will have to settle for the ordinary.' And no one wants to do that!

www.ingramcontent.com/pod-product-compliance
Lightning Source LLC
Chambersburg PA
CBHW072138280526
45788CB00002B/691